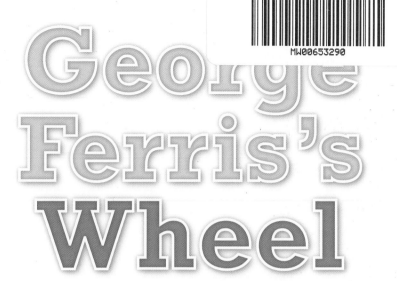

George Ferris's Wheel

by Helen Strahinich

Scott Foresman
is an imprint of

Glenview, Illinois • Boston, Massachusetts • Chandler, Arizona
Upper Saddle River, New Jersey

Illustrations 14, 16 J.T. Morrow

Photographs
Every effort has been made to secure permission and provide appropriate credit for photographic material. The publisher deeply regrets any omission and pledges to correct errors called to its attention in subsequent editions.

Unless otherwise acknowledged, all photographs are the property of Pearson Education, Inc.

Photo locators denoted as follows: Top (T), Center (C), Bottom (B), Left (L), Right (R), Background (Bkgd)

CVR Rommel/Masterfile Corporation; **1** Bettmann/Corbis; **4** Rommel/Masterfile Corporation; **5** Bettmann/Corbis; **6** Kord.com/AGE Fotostock; **7** Daniel Hudson Burnham (1846-1912) 1910 (oil on panel), Hayward, Gerald S. (fl.1910)/© Chicago History Museum, USA/Bridgeman Art Library; **8** The Granger Collection, NY; **9** Corbis; **10** Image courtesy of the Chicago History Museum (ICHi-23825); **12** Corbis; **15** Bettmann/Corbis; **17** B.W. Kilburn/Corbis; **18** Bettmann/Corbis; **19** EyePress/AP Images.

ISBN 13: 978-0-328-52511-9
ISBN 10:   0-328-52511-1

8 9 10 V0FL 16 15 14 13

Table of Contents

Chapter 1

A Fair Idea

There it is! You see the lights around the enormous wheel before you enter the amusement park. It towers over everything.

From the top of the Ferris wheel, you can look out over the whole park. On a clear day, you can see for miles.

Most riders probably don't know the story of the first Ferris wheel. Do you? Do you know why it was built? Do you know how the Ferris wheel got its name?

The Chicago World's Fair of 1893

In 1890, the United States decided to host a world's fair. The fair would mark the 400th anniversary of Christopher Columbus's journey to America.

World's fairs had been held since the mid-1800s. The first world's fair was in London, England. Australia, Austria, and Spain had hosted world's fairs too. The fairs were an opportunity for people from all over the world to see another country's inventions, art, and other attractions.

The United States chose Chicago as the site for the World's Fair of 1893 because it was a leader in business and manufacturing. Chicago also had many of the world's tallest buildings. The United States was becoming wealthy and powerful, and Americans wanted to show off to the world.

The site of the 1893 World's Fair in Chicago

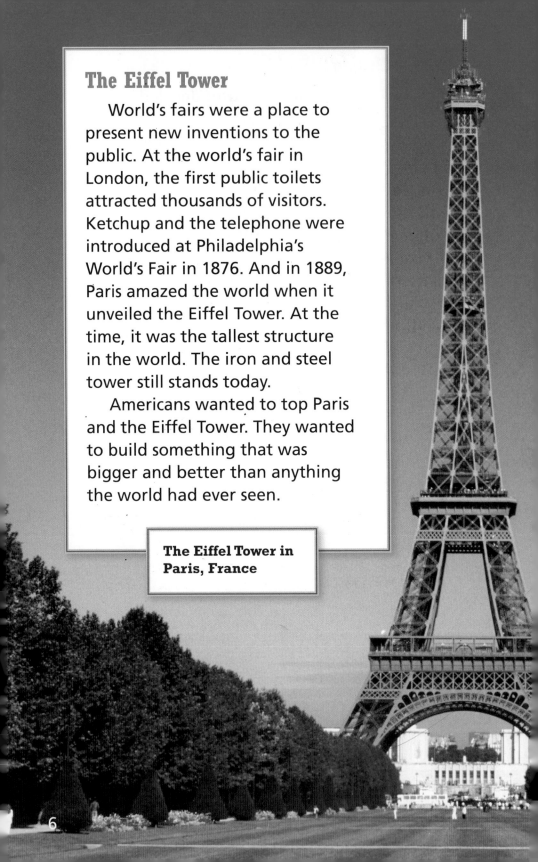

The Eiffel Tower

World's fairs were a place to present new inventions to the public. At the world's fair in London, the first public toilets attracted thousands of visitors. Ketchup and the telephone were introduced at Philadelphia's World's Fair in 1876. And in 1889, Paris amazed the world when it unveiled the Eiffel Tower. At the time, it was the tallest structure in the world. The iron and steel tower still stands today.

Americans wanted to top Paris and the Eiffel Tower. They wanted to build something that was bigger and better than anything the world had ever seen.

The Eiffel Tower in Paris, France

The First Ideas

How could America top the great Eiffel Tower? Many people had ideas. Most called for bigger, taller towers. One person suggested a tower nine times taller than the Eiffel Tower, with an elevator to take visitors to the top and a ramp for them to slide down. Another idea called for a tower made of logs, with a log cabin at the top. Even Mr. Eiffel offered to help by designing another tower!

The fair's chief builder was Daniel Burnham. He was famous for building the country's first skyscrapers—buildings so tall that they seemed to touch the sky. Burnham didn't like the idea of building another tower. He threw out the first ideas of doing that and met with other builders. At the meeting, Burnham asked the builders to think of something new and different.

Daniel Burnham

Chapter 2

George Ferris Thinks Big

George Ferris was part of the team Burnham assembled for the Chicago World's Fair. Ferris's company was in charge of **inspecting** all the steel at the fair. When Ferris heard that Burnham wanted to build something that was new and different, he came up with an idea for a giant wheel.

Ferris didn't waste any time. He sketched out his idea and showed it to Burnham. But Burnham feared that the wheel would not be strong enough. He thought it would be unsafe and that people would be afraid to ride it.

George Ferris came up with an idea to build a big, steel wheel that would hold passengers.

Ferris would not take no for an answer though. He kept working on his idea for a giant wheel. Then he went back to Burnham with more details.

Burnham still wasn't sure about Ferris's wheel. But he couldn't help wondering if Ferris's idea might really work. He showed the **project** to other people. They needed more convincing too.

Everybody was worried that there would be an accident. What would happen to the wheel in a big wind? Would people fall off?

So Ferris went to work again. He collected more information to show that his idea was safe. He even found ways to help pay for it.

This time, Ferris got the go-ahead.

George Ferris's company inspected the construction of steel buildings such as this one at the Chicago World's Fair.

Chapter 3

The Ferris Wheel Goes Up

Ferris faced many challenges while trying to build his wheel. First, the wheel needed a foundation that would secure it into the ground. Building a foundation for the wheel would be difficult in the winter because the ground would be frozen. Second, such a gigantic wheel would take tons of steel. Where would it come from? How would it get to Chicago? Finally, the wheel would need energy to turn. Ferris would need to build a power plant!

Ferris had only four months to build his wheel before the fair was scheduled to open. Could it be done? Could he finish his wheel in time?

Early Critics

Some people said that Ferris's wheel wouldn't work. They thought it would be a failure. Many people said that Ferris was crazy. They called him "The Man with Wheels in his Head." But that didn't stop Ferris.

Setting the Foundation

Ferris wanted the wheel to be huge. It needed a strong foundation to keep it standing. Construction began in January, just as Chicago was experiencing its coldest winter on record. Workers used dynamite to break through the frozen ground. Then they thawed the ground with steam so that they could dig eight holes for steel beams and cement. The steam pumps ran day and night. Each hole had to be 20 feet wide, 20 feet long, and 35 feet deep.

Because the 1893 World's Fair was built on this land in Chicago, George Ferris knew a strong foundation would be absolutely necessary for his giant wheel.

Building the Wheel

With time running out, Ferris and his crew worked hard and fast. Nine different steel mills in Detroit, Michigan, made most of the 100,000 separate parts of the wheel. Then the steel was shipped to Chicago by train to be put together there. Each part had to be placed perfectly. Any mistake could be deadly.

At the same time, two coal-fired steam engines were being built 700 feet away from where the wheel would stand. One engine would be used to power the wheel. The second engine would be used if the first one broke down.

When the Chicago World's Fair opened in May 1893, the wheel was not quite complete. Ferris needed to finish the job quickly, and his work had to be perfect.

Nine different steel mills made most of the 100,000 separate parts for the first Ferris wheel.

The Wheel Turns

On June 9, 1893, workers finally tested the wheel. The passenger cars were not attached yet. The workers turned on the power and watched as the wheel made one complete turn. Onlookers cheered and **applauded.**

Two days later, a few passengers took a ride. Among the first passengers were Daniel Burnham and Ferris's wife, Margaret. People who worried about safety could now believe that Ferris's wheel was safe. The Ferris wheel was finally ready to be presented to the public!

Chapter 4

A Giant Hit

Americans flocked to the Ferris wheel. During the ride, passengers could look over the fairgrounds and see Lake Michigan. On a clear day, they could glimpse four states: Illinois, Indiana, Michigan, and Wisconsin.

The Ferris wheel was the fair's most popular attraction. The cost of a ride was fifty cents. Each of the 36 cars could hold 60 passengers—that's 2,160 passengers at a time! In the six months that the fair ran, nearly 1.5 million people rode the great Ferris wheel. And the wheel ran without any trouble.

The Ferris wheel helped to make the fair a success. Chicago's fair attracted more than 27 million people. Two hundred new structures were built on the grounds, which covered more than six hundred acres.

The view from inside a car of the Ferris wheel.

Love at First Sight

People loved the Ferris wheel. Maybe it was the wonderful view. Or maybe it was the **fabulous** invention itself. The wheel was 250 feet across, and the cars at the top went up 264 feet. Its 3,000 blinking light bulbs made it appear magical at night. No matter what other attractions the crowds were **browsing,** they could always look up to see the magnificent machine.

Some couples even wanted to get married on the Ferris wheel. That was not allowed. However, a few did get married nearby.

Entrance to the Ferris wheel.

St. Louis
World's Fair
in 1904.

After the Fair

When the Chicago fair ended in late October 1893, no one knew what to do with the giant Ferris wheel. Some people said it should be moved to New York City, but the cost was too high.

So the Ferris wheel stayed on the fairgrounds all winter. In 1895, Ferris found a new site. The wheel was set up on Chicago's North Side, across from Lincoln Park.

Then, in 1904, the Ferris wheel was set up again for the St. Louis World's Fair. After that fair, too, people wondered what to do with it.

The great Ferris wheel stood rusting in St. Louis for two years. It became an eyesore. Finally, the pride of two world's fairs was destroyed with dynamite, and it crashed to the ground.

Although the original Ferris wheel is gone, thousands are still in use. Builders have improved on the original idea. They have built Ferris wheels in many different sizes. Some models swing. Others turn upside down. The tallest Ferris wheel is in Jiangxi, China. At over five hundred feet, it is nearly twice the size of Ferris's original wheel. And larger wheels may soon be built.

The story of the first great rides on the giant wheel is worth remembering. Ferris's invention has inspired millions of people. In 1893 there was nothing quite like it. Some people think that's still true today.

The Star of Nanchang is the tallest Ferris wheel in the world.

Glossary

applauded v. showed approval by clapping the hands, shouting, etc.

browsing v. looking here and there

fabulous adj. wonderful; exciting

inspecting v. looking over carefully; examining

project n. a plan; effort; undertaking